The Wisdom of Isaac Luria: Tzimtzum, Tikkun, and the Kabbalistic Blueprint of the Universe

ISBN: 9798291695876

Chapters

Why Isaac Luria Still Matters

Why is the world the way it is? Why does a universe seemingly born of divine intelligence contain so much chaos, pain, and fragmentation? We live in a reality of breathtaking beauty and unspeakable cruelty, of profound connection and desolate loneliness. We sense a deeper order, a cosmic blueprint, yet we are confronted daily by evidence of its fracture. This is not a new question. It is the perennial cry of the human soul, whispered in ancient temples and shouted in modern streets: If there is a source of infinite goodness, why is the world so broken? And, perhaps more urgently, what is my role in it all?

Five centuries ago, in the windswept, mystical city of Safed, a teacher appeared who offered one of the most radical, daring, and ultimately hopeful answers to this question ever conceived. His name was Isaac Luria, but he would come to be known by a title of reverence and awe: the *Ari*, "the Holy Lion." In a teaching career that lasted less than three years, the Ari did not just reinterpret the ancient mystical tradition of Kabbalah; he detonated it, reassembling the pieces into a new and electrifying vision of the cosmos. He gave us a story of God, the universe, and ourselves—a story of cosmic contraction, catastrophic shattering, and the sacred duty of repair.

This book is an invitation into that story. It is a guide to the wisdom of Isaac Luria, a man who became the architect of a new mystical consciousness. Luria's cosmology is not a gentle, linear unfolding of divine perfection. It is a dynamic, volatile, and participatory drama. It begins not with a simple "Let there be light," but with a profound paradox: for anything to exist, the Infinite—what Kabbalists call *Ein Sof*—had to first withdraw, creating a space for a finite world. This primal act of divine self-limitation, known as *Tzimtzum*, is the ultimate expression of cosmic humility. It is an act of making room.

But this process was fraught with peril. Into this conceptual void, God emanated a brilliant light, meant to be held and structured by a series of divine "vessels," the *Sefirot*. But the light was too powerful, the vessels too brittle. They shattered. This is the second act of the cosmic drama, the *Shevirat ha-Kelim*, the Shattering of the Vessels. This is Luria's breathtaking explanation for the state of our world. The world is broken because it was *born* from a shattering. The very fabric of reality is woven from the shards of these primordial vessels. And, crucially, scattered among these shards are holy sparks of divine light, now fallen, trapped, and exiled within the material world.

This is where humanity enters the stage. For Luria, we are not merely fallen creatures living in a broken world, lamenting our exile from Eden. We are the solution. The third and final act of the drama is *Tikkun Olam*, the Repair of the World. And it is our life's work. The Ari taught that every human being is born with a sacred mission: to find, uplift, and restore the fallen sparks of divine light hidden within our reality. Through our conscious actions, our focused intentions, our ethical choices, and even our struggles, we become partners with God in the mending of creation. Every act of kindness, every focused prayer, every moment of genuine connection is an act of cosmic restoration.

This is the profound and empowering core of Luria's wisdom. He provides a framework that gives meaning to our existence, context to our suffering, and urgency to our moral lives. Your personal struggles are not isolated events; they are part of the *tikkun* of your own unique soul. The fragmentation you see in society is not a sign of God's absence, but a call to your sacred responsibility. The Ari's vision transforms the universe from a static backdrop into a living, breathing entity that feels our every action and responds to our deepest intentions.

This book, therefore, is more than an exploration of historical ideas. It is a practical guide to a new way of seeing and being. It is about learning to perceive the hidden sparks in the everyday, to understand the spiritual mechanics of reality, and to actively participate in its healing. From the architecture of the soul and the cycles of reincarnation to the mystical power of intention and the feminine presence of God, Luria's teachings provide a comprehensive blueprint of the unseen world. He offers us not a faith of passive acceptance, but a spirituality of radical responsibility.

The wisdom of the Holy Lion of Safed has echoed through the centuries, shaping entire spiritual movements and inspiring seekers far beyond his own time and place. Today, in an age of global anxiety and profound disconnection, his message is more relevant than ever. He tells us that the world is not broken by accident, but by design, so that we might have the sublime honor of becoming its healers. Let us now begin the journey into this blueprint of the universe, to learn the story of its shattering and, most importantly, to discover our part in its magnificent repair.

How to Read This Book

The teachings of Isaac Luria are not a conventional philosophy to be grasped by the intellect alone. They are a visionary map of the hidden dimensions of reality, a system transmitted from a master mystic to his chosen disciple. To engage with Lurianic Kabbalah is to enter a world where metaphor and metaphysics merge, where psychological insights are presented as cosmic events, and where every letter of a sacred text is a portal to a deeper truth. Therefore, reading this book requires a particular mindset—a balance between intellectual rigor and contemplative openness.

First, approach these concepts as you would a complex piece of music or a profound poem. Allow the central images to work on your imagination. Picture the infinite, undifferentiated light of *Ein Sof*. Visualize its withdrawal, the *Tzimtzum*, creating a sphere of potential. Feel the catastrophic drama of the *Shevirah*, the Shattering of the Vessels, and see the sparks of light cascading into the darkness. This is not merely mythology; for the Kabbalist, this is the deep structure of reality. Engaging with the ideas on an intuitive and imaginative level is as important as understanding them logically.

Second, this book is built around the three foundational pillars of the Lurianic system. You will encounter them again and again, each time with a deeper layer of meaning:

1. *Tzimtzum* **(Contraction):** The primal act of divine self-limitation that allowed the universe to come into being. It is the cosmic source of "making space."

2. *Shevirah* **(Shattering):** The primordial catastrophe where the vessels meant to contain the divine light broke, resulting in the fragmented, exiled state of our world.

3. *Tikkun* **(Repair/Rectification):** The sacred task, assigned primarily to humanity, of gathering the scattered sparks of divine light and restoring cosmic harmony.

Think of these three concepts as a recurring motif. Each chapter will explore them from a different angle—historical, cosmological, psychological, or practical. By the end of the book, these terms should not just be definitions you have memorized, but lenses through which you can view the world and your own life.

Finally, you will find many Hebrew terms throughout these pages. They are retained not to be obscure, but because they hold a universe of meaning that is often lost in translation. *Tzimtzum*, for example, means more than just "contraction"; it carries echoes of concentration, concealment, and stepping back. Do not be intimidated by these words. They are signposts pointing to deep concepts. A comprehensive Glossary is provided at the end of this book to serve as your constant companion and guide. Use it frequently to refresh your memory and deepen your understanding.

A Note on Sources and Interpretation

Reading the wisdom of Isaac Luria presents a unique and fascinating challenge: the Ari himself wrote almost nothing. Aside from a few poems and commentaries, he committed virtually none of his revolutionary system to paper. He believed his teachings were part of the *Torah she-be`al peh*, the Oral Law—a living, breathing wisdom that could only be transmitted soul to soul, from the mouth of the master to the ear of the disciple. Writing, he felt, would freeze this dynamic flow, reducing a torrent of divine insight into a static artifact.

Consequently, everything we know of Luria's intricate cosmology, his meditative practices, and his vision of the soul comes to us through the pen of his foremost student, Rabbi Ḥayyim Vital

(1542-1620). For the brief period the Ari taught in Safed, Vital was his shadow, his scribe, his living repository. He transcribed Luria's discourses, recorded his answers to complex questions, and documented his master's mystical practices with meticulous care. After Luria's untimely death, it was Vital who took on the sacred and monumental task of organizing this vast body of material into a coherent system. The result was a collection of writings, most famously the eight "gates" or volumes that culminate in *Etz Hayyim* ("The Tree of Life"), which form the bedrock of Lurianic Kabbalah.

This fact is crucial for our interpretation. When we read "Luria's teachings," we are, in fact, reading Vital's transmission of those teachings. We are seeing the light of the Ari through the lens of Vital's own brilliant but distinct consciousness. This is not a flaw in the transmission; within the Kabbalistic tradition, it is its very nature. Wisdom is never received passively; it is always filtered through, and shaped by, the vessel of the student. We are therefore engaging with a beautiful and complex dialogue between two extraordinary minds. Our journey into the Ari's wisdom is guided by the hand of the one man he trusted to preserve it for all time.

A Light Born in Safed

To understand the explosive emergence of Isaac Luria, one must first understand the city that became his stage: Safed. Perched high in the green, windswept mountains of the Upper Galilee, 16th-century Safed was more than a city; it was a crucible of spiritual longing. In the wake of the catastrophic expulsion of the Jews from Spain in 1492, a collective trauma that shattered communities and upended a golden age of Jewish life, Safed became a beacon. Under the relatively stable and tolerant rule of the Ottoman Empire, it drew scholars, poets, and mystics from across the diaspora. They came to this city, suspended between heaven and earth, to be near the ancient tombs of sages and prophets, most notably that of Rabbi Shimon bar Yochai, the reputed author of the Kabbalah's foundational text, the Zohar.

The air in Safed was thick with messianic yearning and an urgent desire to make sense of suffering and exile. This was not a theoretical question; it was the lived reality of a generation of refugees. Why had this calamity befallen them? What was the divine meaning of their dispersal? Kabbalah, the ancient tradition of Jewish mysticism, provided the tools to answer these questions. The city hummed with mystical energy. Groups of Kabbalists—*chaverim*, or "friends"—would gather to study texts, practice meditative techniques, and embark on spiritual journeys. They performed ritual immersions in the city's cold springs, confessed their sins publicly to one another, and welcomed the Sabbath in the fields, singing to a mystical bride. It was into this supercharged environment, a "golden age" of Jewish mysticism, that Isaac Luria arrived like a spark landing in a bed of dry tinder.

His own life was a tapestry woven from the diverse threads of the Jewish world. Born in Jerusalem around 1534, his father was an Ashkenazi Jew of German or Polish descent, while his mother was from a Sephardic family. After his father's early death, the young Isaac and his mother moved to Egypt, where he was raised in the home of his wealthy uncle, a tax farmer. By all accounts, he was a prodigy. He quickly mastered rabbinic literature and Talmudic law, displaying a brilliant and incisive intellect that could have secured him a comfortable life as a respected legal scholar.

But a different calling was stirring within him. As a young man, he grew increasingly drawn to the esoteric mysteries of the Zohar. He obtained a rare, handwritten copy and began to spend his days in intense study. Eventually, he retreated into a life of near-total seclusion, spending years on a small, quiet island on the Nile River that was owned by his father-in-law. For seven years, he would remain in isolation six days a week, returning to his family only for the Sabbath. It was here, in the silence and solitude of the Nile, poring over the cryptic Aramaic of the Zohar, that Luria's unique mystical vision began to form. Later traditions claim that it was during this period that he was visited by the prophet Elijah, who revealed to him the deepest secrets of the cosmos, the doctrine that would become Lurianic Kabbalah.

Around 1570, guided by what he felt was a divine command, Luria left Egypt and made his way to the heart of the Kabbalistic world: Safed. He was 36 years old. When he arrived, the city's mystical life was dominated by the towering figure of Rabbi Moses Cordovero, known as the Ramak. Cordovero was a brilliant systematizer, a man who had taken the vast, sprawling traditions of Kabbalah and organized them into a coherent, encyclopedic whole. His system described a logical, orderly process of emanation, explaining how the infinite, perfect Godhead unfolded itself, step by step, through the ten *Sefirot* to create a perfect world. Cordovero's Kabbalah was a majestic, rational explanation of divine unfolding.

Luria's was a bolt of lightning from another sky. He did not come to debate Cordovero's system; he came to offer a radical alternative. Where Cordovero saw order, Luria saw drama and catastrophe. His central concern was not how a perfect world was emanated, but why the world we experience is so clearly imperfect and broken. He possessed an otherworldly charisma and, it was said, supernatural abilities—the power to read faces and see the spiritual history of a person's soul, to understand the language of birds, and to perceive the souls of long-dead sages lingering in the Galilean fields.

A small circle of Safed's most advanced mystics, including the young and brilliant Ḥayyim Vital, were drawn to him irresistibly. Then, in a pivotal moment of history, just weeks or months after Luria's arrival, Moses Cordovero died. Legend holds that at his funeral, a pillar of fire was seen, and a voice declared that Luria was to be his successor. The mantle of leadership passed from the great systematizer to the radical visionary.

The Ari's teaching career in Safed was breathtakingly brief—less than three years, from sometime in 1570 until his untimely death in an epidemic in the summer of 1572. He was only 38 years old. Yet in that short span, he revolutionized

Jewish mysticism for all time. He did not lecture in a formal academy. Instead, he would walk with his small, handpicked circle of disciples through the fields and vineyards surrounding the city, revealing the secret life of the universe. He would point to a tree, a stone, or a spring and explain the reincarnated soul dwelling within it and the *tikkun*, the spiritual repair, it was waiting to complete. His teachings were not abstract lectures but living revelations, transmitted orally and spontaneously, tailored to the souls of the men who were present. It was an incandescent, almost frantic period of transmission, as if Luria knew his time was short. His death left his followers with a powerful, fragmented, and urgent inheritance—a blueprint for a cosmos shattered, waiting to be repaired.

Ḥayyim Vital and the Transmission of the Teachings

The wisdom of Isaac Luria is a light that reaches us through a single, indispensable lens: his student, Rabbi Ḥayyim Vital. To approach the Ari's thought is to encounter one of the most profound and symbiotic master-disciple relationships in the history of mysticism. Without Vital, the Ari would be a ghost, a legend of Safed whispered about in esoteric circles, his revolutionary cosmology lost to the winds of the Galilee. It was Vital who served as the conduit, the living repository, and the architectural memory for a system of thought so vast and complex it threatened to vanish the moment its creator passed from the world.

Ḥayyim Vital was no mere secretary. He was a formidable Kabbalist in his own right, a man of intense spiritual ambition and discipline. Before meeting Luria, he had studied with the great Moses Cordovero and was already a respected figure in Safed's mystical circles. Yet, upon encountering the Ari, Vital recognized he was in the presence of a different order of soul entirely. He understood almost immediately that his life's purpose had been revealed: to become the vessel for Luria's revelation. He attached himself to the Ari with absolute devotion, documenting every discourse, every private conversation, every seemingly casual remark that contained a kernel of mystical truth. He saw himself not as an author but as a divine scribe, entrusted with a sacred task of cosmic importance.

The transmission process was jealously guarded. Luria's teachings were not meant for public consumption. They were considered potent, even dangerous, containing mysteries that could destabilize an unprepared mind. The Ari's small circle of disciples was sworn to secrecy, forbidden from transcribing his words for anyone else. Vital, however, was the exception. He was the designated scribe, the one tasked with capturing the torrent of oral teachings. His writings were initially for his own use, personal notebooks filled with frantic scribbles trying to keep pace with the Ari's flowing, spontaneous revelations. After Luria's death, Vital understood his personal notes were now a sacred inheritance. He spent the rest of his life organizing, editing, and systematizing this vast, chaotic, and brilliant collection of material into a coherent structure.

This brings us to a central mystery: why did Luria himself refuse to write? In a world of scholars, his near-total lack of written output is a profound statement. This refusal was not an oversight; it was a core element of his mystical philosophy. First, he believed that to commit his teachings to paper would be to betray their very nature. Divine wisdom, for Luria, was a *shefa*, a living, dynamic flow. It was an energy that could not be pinned down, classified, and killed by the static and finite nature of the written word. A book presents information; a true master transmits life.

Second, the act of writing freezes a teaching that should be fluid and adaptable. Luria tailored his lessons to the specific soul-root and spiritual capacity of the person before him. A teaching given to one disciple might be subtly different from one given to another, because their paths of *tikkun*, or spiritual repair, were different. A book, by contrast, is a monologue; it cannot gaze into the soul of the reader and adjust its message accordingly. Oral transmission, from master to disciple, was the only way to ensure the wisdom was received in a way that was both safe and efficacious. His refusal to write was, in its own way, a form of *tzimtzum*, a self-contraction to make space for the vital role of the disciple and the sacred, living relationship between them.

From Vital's monumental efforts, the Lurianic corpus was born. Though other disciples also kept notes, it was Vital's version that became the authorized canon. He structured the teachings into a series of "gates," each one a portal into a different aspect of the Ari's cosmology. The culmination of this work is the masterpiece known as *Etz Ḥayyim* ("The Tree of Life"), a dense and sprawling work that maps the spiritual DNA of the universe. It, along with other related texts compiled by Vital and his son, Shmuel, forms the foundation of all subsequent Lurianic Kabbalah. When we study the Ari's blueprint of the universe, we are walking through a palace whose foundation was laid by Luria, but whose every stone was measured, cut, and placed by the faithful hands of Ḥayyim Vital.

The Ari's Enduring Influence

Though his teaching career was a mere flicker in time, the light of Isaac Luria's vision projected itself across the centuries, fundamentally reshaping the landscape of Jewish thought and leaving an indelible mark on the broader world of mysticism. The Ari did not simply add a new chapter to the book of Kabbalah; he provided a new language and a new lens through which the entire tradition would henceforth be read. His ideas were so powerful and so resonant with the spiritual anxieties of the age that they quickly eclipsed the more staid, systematic Kabbalah of his predecessor, Moses Cordovero. Lurianic Kabbalah became, for all intents and purposes, *the* Kabbalah.

Its immediate impact was revolutionary. Later Kabbalists, particularly in the 17th and 18th centuries, dedicated themselves almost exclusively to studying, interpreting, and expanding upon the writings of Ḥayyim Vital. The Ari's cosmology became the essential framework for understanding the Zohar and all prior mystical texts. His concepts provided a compelling metaphysical explanation for the continued exile (*galut*) of the Jewish people. It was no longer seen as a mere punishment for sin, but as a reflection of a cosmic state of brokenness—a divine exile in which the people were called to participate in a sacred mission of repair. This transformed the experience of suffering from a passive state of endurance into an active, meaningful, and redemptive vocation.

Perhaps the most significant and far-reaching impact of Lurianic thought was its role as the seedbed for the Hasidic movement, which swept through Eastern Europe in the 18th century. The founder of Hasidism, Rabbi Israel ben Eliezer, known as the Baal Shem Tov ("Master of the Good Name"), took the core concepts of Luria's elite, esoteric system and democratized them, turning them into a mass spiritual revival.

The Lurianic idea of *nitzotzot*, the holy sparks hidden in all material things, became the Hasidic belief that divinity can be found everywhere, even in the most mundane aspects of life. The act of eating a meal, telling a story, or doing business could become a holy act of *tikkun*, of raising the sparks. The Ari's emphasis on *kavvanah*, the power of focused intention, was transformed into the Hasidic ideal of *devekut*, a constant, cleaving devotion to God in every moment. The complex, theurgical meditations of the Safed Kabbalists were simplified into the heartfelt, ecstatic prayer of the common person. Hasidism took the Ari's cosmic drama of Shattering and Repair and placed it directly into the hands and hearts of the people, making every individual a key player in the story of redemption.

But the Ari's influence did not stop at the borders of the Jewish world. As Kabbalah began to seep into Western consciousness, particularly from the Renaissance onward, Luria's ideas proved to be magnetic for non-Jewish thinkers as well. Christian Kabbalists and, later, Western esotericists and occult philosophers were fascinated by his intricate cosmology, his vision of a dynamic and interactive divinity, and his model of cosmic evolution through catastrophe and restoration. Though often misunderstood or stripped of their specific Jewish context, Lurianic concepts can be seen echoing in the works of figures like the German idealist philosophers and, later, in the psychological theories of Carl Jung, with his focus on fragmentation and integration.

Today, the Ari's legacy is more accessible than ever. In a remarkable journey from the secretive circles of 16th-century Safed to the global network of the 21st century, his teachings have entered cyberspace. Websites, online courses, and digital libraries have made the texts of *Etz Hayyim* available to a global audience of spiritual seekers. Concepts like *Tikkun Olam* have entered the popular lexicon, often used to describe social and environmental activism. This modern interpretation speaks to the enduring power of Luria's central idea: that the world is a broken but sacred place, and that we, its inhabitants, are endowed with the power and the responsibility to mend it. The Holy Lion of Safed is no longer just a figure of historical interest; his wisdom continues to provide a profound and urgent blueprint for finding meaning in a fragmented world.

Tzimtzum: The Contraction of Divine Light

Before anything could be—before light, time, matter, or consciousness—there was a profound philosophical problem. It is the ultimate paradox that has haunted theologians and metaphysicians for millennia: If God is infinite, all-encompassing, and perfect, how can a world possibly exist? If the divine reality, which the Kabbalists call *Ein Sof* ("Without End"), is truly everywhere, filling every conceivable and inconceivable dimension, then there is no "outside," no empty space, no blank canvas upon which a universe could be painted. How does the Something emerge from the All? How can a finite and imperfect world come into being from a source of infinite perfection?

Prior Kabbalistic systems, like that of Moses Cordovero, described creation as a linear process of emanation, a gentle overflowing of divine goodness, like a spring bubbling over. But for Isaac Luria, this didn't solve the core paradox. An overflowing still implies that the spring and the water are of the same essence. It could not explain the radical *otherness* of our world, its perceived separation from God, its capacity for darkness and brokenness. Luria's genius was to propose a solution of breathtaking originality. He taught that the first act of creation was not an act of expression, but an act of concealment. It was not an overflowing, but a withdrawal. This primordial act is called *Tzimtzum*.

Before the beginning, there was only *Ein Sof*. It is crucial to understand that *Ein Sof* is not "God" in the personal, relational sense. It is the absolute, undifferentiated ground of all being. Imagine not a light source, but Light itself—infinite, homogenous, without center or periphery, without quality or attribute, for attributes would imply limitation. It is a state of pure, limitless potential, so complete and so total that nothing else *is*. In this plenum of divine light, there is no here or there, no now or then, no self or other. There is only the seamless, endless reality of the Infinite. For a world to exist, a world defined by its finitude, its boundaries, and its separateness, a conceptual space had to be cleared.

Here we arrive at the first movement in the cosmic drama. The Ari taught that in order to bring forth creation, *Ein Sof* performed the *Tzimtzum*: a contraction, a withdrawal, a pulling-in of its own infinite light. Imagine the Infinite withdrawing "from itself into itself," creating a spherical, conceptual "void" or "vacated space" (*tehiru* in Aramaic) within its own being. This was not a physical act happening in some pre-existing space; this act *created the very possibility of space*. It was an act of divine imagination, a self-limitation of staggering proportions. The void was not an absolute nothingness, for nothing can be truly separate from *Ein Sof*. Rather, it was a region where the infinite light, while still present, was profoundly concealed, allowing for a reality of a lower, finite order to take root and exist without being instantly re-absorbed into the infinite. The *Tzimtzum* is the divine exhale that makes room for the universe. It is the ultimate act of making space.

This radical idea is the key that unlocks the rest of Luria's system, but it is not a simple concept with a single meaning. The power of *Tzimtzum* lies in its multiple layers of interpretation, which range from the cosmic to the deeply personal.

First, *Tzimtzum* can be understood as a literal, cosmic event. In this view, the contraction is the foundational event of cosmogony, the metaphysical "Big Bang" that preceded the physical one. It is the story of how God cleared a space within Himself to serve as the stage for the subsequent drama of creation, shattering, and repair. This interpretation gives us the grand, mythological framework of Lurianic Kabbalah. It posits that the universe exists within a sphere of divine concealment, a bubble of finitude floating in the sea of the Infinite.

Second, *Tzimtzum* can be read as a powerful metaphor for divine self-limitation. This more philosophical interpretation suggests that the "contraction" is not a literal event but a metaphor for God's choice to restrain His omnipotence and omniscience to allow for the existence of free will and genuine otherness. For creation to be more than a divine puppet show, it must have the capacity for independent action, for choice, and even for error. For this to be possible, God must, in an act of supreme love and grace, hold back the full, overwhelming force of His presence. *Tzimtzum* is the divine humility that allows the created being to stand on its own feet, to enter into a real relationship with its creator.

Third, and perhaps most relevant for the modern seeker, *Tzimtzum* is a psychological and ethical model for human behavior. The Ari's cosmic blueprint doubles as a guide for the soul. If the first act of the divine was to make space for the other, then this becomes our own highest spiritual practice. In a conversation, *tzimtzum* is the act of contracting one's own ego and agenda to truly listen, to create a space where the other person can express themselves without being judged or interrupted. In a relationship, it is the humility to allow your partner, your child, or your friend the room to grow, to make their own mistakes, and to become who they are meant to be. In spiritual life, it is the practice of quieting the inner noise of the self to make room for the sacred, for the subtle voice of the soul to be heard.

The doctrine of *Tzimtzum* teaches a profound lesson: creation, whether cosmic or personal, begins not with assertion, but with withdrawal. It is born from the holy and generative power of empty space. This single, revolutionary concept sets the stage for everything that is to follow: the fragile vessels that will form in this new space, the brilliant light that will pour into them, and the catastrophic shattering that is to come.

The Primordial Vessels and Their Shattering

The act of *Tzimtzum* set the stage. Within the infinite reality of *Ein Sof*, a conceptual void (*tehiru*) now existed—a sphere of profound divine concealment, pregnant with the potential for a finite world. But this void was not left empty. The cosmic drama did not end with God's withdrawal. On the contrary, it was only the beginning. For a world to be built, it needed not just space, but also structure and substance. Luria taught that after the contraction, a single, thin ray of divine light, a *kav*, penetrated the vacated space. It pierced the void like a beam of light entering a dark room, serving as a conduit, a channel from the infinite light source of *Ein Sof* into the heart of the newly formed potentiality.

This ray of light did not simply flood the void. Its purpose was to organize it, to give it form and definition. As the *kav* extended downwards into the void, it brought with it the blueprint for creation: the ten *Sefirot*. The *Sefirot* are the fundamental archetypes of existence, the divine emanations or attributes through which the infinite Godhead interacts with and manifests in the finite world. They are often depicted as a "Tree of Life," representing qualities like Wisdom (*Chokhmah*), Understanding (*Binah*), Loving-kindness (*Chesed*), Judgment (*Gevurah*), and Beauty (*Tiferet*). In this initial stage of creation, known as the World of *Tohu* (Chaos), the *Sefirot* manifested as a series of distinct points, or vessels (*kelim*). Each *sefirah* was created as a container, designed to receive, hold, and transmit a specific quality of the divine light flowing down the *kav*. The plan was perfect: a series of ten vessels, arranged in a linear sequence, ready to be filled with light, forming the stable skeleton of a perfect universe.

Here, the cosmic drama takes a catastrophic turn. The light from *Ein Sof* continued to pour through the *kav*, streaming into the newly formed vessels. The first three vessels—Crown (*Keter*), Wisdom (*Chokhmah*), and Understanding (*Binah*)—being of a higher, more subtle nature, were able to withstand the influx. But as the torrent of light reached the lower seven vessels, a disaster of cosmic proportions occurred. They were too fragile, too rigid, too immature to contain the sheer intensity of the divine influx. They were vessels of separation, each one designed to hold its own specific quality of light in isolation. But the light itself was a holistic, unified, and infinitely powerful force. The vessels could not handle the pressure. One by one, they broke.

This is the central event of the Lurianic cosmogony: *Shevirat ha-Kelim*, the Shattering of the Vessels. It is the primal catastrophe that occurred at the dawn of time, the cosmic birth trauma that defines the very nature of our reality. Imagine delicate clay pots being filled with a torrent of molten metal; they burst apart. The structures designed to give order to the universe were overwhelmed and destroyed by the very divine energy they were meant to contain. The result was not a failure of God's plan, but a necessary, if cataclysmic, stage in it. The world born of simple, linear perfection was too brittle. A different, more complex and resilient reality had to be forged from its ruins.

When the vessels shattered, two things happened. First, the divine light they contained was released. But it was no longer a single, coherent beam. It was fragmented into an infinite number of holy sparks, the *nitzotzot*. These sparks of pure divinity, exiled from their source, cascaded down into the void, scattered throughout the lowest depths of reality. They are the hidden, inner life of creation, points of sacred potential buried within the material world. Second, the broken pieces of the vessels themselves also fell. These are the shards, the shells, known as the *kelippot*. Unlike the sparks, which are pure light and holiness, the *kelippot* are the source of all that is coarse, opaque, and dark in the universe. They are the husks of holiness, containers that have lost their inner light and are now defined by their hardness, their separateness, and their ability to conceal and entrap the sacred sparks.

This brings us to the profound Lurianic diagnosis of our world. The reality we inhabit is a chaotic mixture of these two primordial elements. Everything that exists—every human being, every animal, every plant, every stone, every thought, every emotion—is a composite of holy sparks (*nitzotzot*) trapped within a shell of materiality (*kelippot*). This is why the world is a place of such maddening paradox. We see breathtaking beauty next to grotesque ugliness; we feel profound love and bitter hatred; we experience moments of transcendent clarity and periods of soul-crushing darkness. This is because everything is a battlefield. Within every created thing, a divine spark yearns to return to its source, while the shard that encases it pulls it down, concealing its light. The world is not inherently evil; it is broken. It is a universe in exile from itself, filled with scattered light waiting to be gathered.

And the responsibility for that sacred gathering, as we shall see, falls to humanity.

Tikkun Olam: The Cosmic and Human Repair

The cosmic stage is now set. The primordial reality, born of divine withdrawal (*Tzimtzum*) and shattered at its inception (*Shevirah*), is a landscape of holy ruins. The universe is a mixture of light and shadow, of sacred sparks (*nitzotzot*) imprisoned within broken shards (*kelippot*). This is the world we have inherited—a world of exile, fragmentation, and hidden divinity. A lesser cosmology might end here, presenting a tragic myth of a failed creation. But for Isaac Luria, this catastrophe was not the end of the story. It was the necessary prelude to the true purpose of existence. The shattering was not a mistake; it was the event that made our lives meaningful. It created the very possibility of the third and final act of the cosmic drama: *Tikkun Olam*, the Repair of the World.

If the *Tzimtzum* was God's act and the *Shevirah* was a cosmic process, the *Tikkun* is fundamentally a human task. This is the most radical and empowering element of the Ari's wisdom. Humanity is not a helpless bystander in a flawed creation. We are not simply fallen creatures, cursed to wander in the wreckage of a primordial disaster. On the contrary, we are the principal agents of restoration. Luria teaches that humanity was created specifically for this purpose. We are placed at the nexus of the spiritual and physical realms, uniquely equipped to perform the sacred work of mending the cosmos. We are, in a profound sense, God's partners in the completion of creation. The world was intentionally left unfinished so that we could have the honor of finishing it.

The work of *Tikkun* is the slow, patient, and deliberate process of raising the fallen sparks. This is not a metaphor; for the Kabbalist, it is the deepest metaphysical truth of our actions. The divine sparks that were scattered during the *Shevirah* became trapped in the material world—in our food, our possessions, our relationships, our bodies, and our thoughts. They are the inner life-force of all things, but they are in exile, yearning to be liberated from their shells and returned to their divine source. The process of liberation is the central mission of the human soul. Every time we perform an action with the right consciousness, we become a spiritual catalyst. We break open a shard, release the spark within, and assist its ascent back to the higher worlds, thus contributing to the mending of the divine fabric.

This principle transforms the entirety of human life into a spiritual practice of cosmic significance. Suddenly, every act matters. Eating a piece of fruit is no longer a simple biological function; it is an opportunity. By making a blessing over the fruit with focused intention, we can separate the divine spark of life-energy within it from its physical shell, elevating the spark while we receive physical nourishment. Engaging in business ethically, speaking a word of kindness, resisting a negative impulse, or studying a sacred text—all these become acts of *tikkun*. Luria's vision infuses the mundane with the miraculous. The kitchen, the marketplace, and the study hall become workshops for the repair of the universe. We are constantly surrounded by fallen light, and our lives are a continuous series of opportunities to redeem it.

The essential ingredient in this spiritual alchemy is *kavvanah*, or focused intention. It is not merely the physical act that performs the *tikkun*, but the consciousness behind it. An act performed mechanically, without awareness, has little or no power to elevate the sparks. It is the focused, loving, and directed intention of the human heart and mind that acts as the spiritual laser, capable of piercing the *kelippot*. *Kavvanah* is the dance of intention and rectification. It is the conscious alignment of one's inner world with the divine purpose of an action. When we pray, we are not just reciting words; with proper *kavvanah*, we are channeling divine energies, reconfiguring the spiritual worlds, and facilitating the ascent of the fallen sparks.

This is the heroic and hopeful core of the Ari's wisdom. It provides a profound answer to the problem of suffering and evil. The world is broken because that brokenness is our field of action. Our purpose is not to lament the darkness, but to find the particles of light hidden within it. We are not here to passively await a redemption that will be delivered from on high. We are here to actively build that redemption, one spark at a time, through the sacred work of our everyday lives.

The Soul's Anatomy: Nefesh, Ruach, and Neshamah

In the Lurianic vision, the maxim "As above, so below" is a foundational truth. The cosmic architecture of the Five Worlds is not just an external reality; it is mirrored precisely in the interior structure of the human being. The soul is not a simple, indivisible ghost in the machine of the body. It is a multi-dimensional consciousness, a luminous ladder connecting our physical actions on earth to the highest realms of divine unity. To understand our mission of *tikkun*, we must first understand the anatomy of the instrument that performs it: the soul itself. Luria teaches that the soul is primarily composed of a tripartite structure, three distinct levels of consciousness that correspond directly to the three lower worlds of Creation, Formation, and Action.

The most accessible level of the soul, the one most intimately connected to the body, is the **Nefesh**. This is the vital or "animal" soul. The *Nefesh* is the engine of our physical existence. It animates the body, governs our instincts, drives our biological urges, and fuels our actions. Its consciousness is rooted in the body's experience: sensation, movement, and survival. Spiritually, the *Nefesh* corresponds to the lowest world, **Asiyah**, the World of Action. It is the part of our soul that lives and operates in the physical realm, and its primary mode of expression is through doing. The *tikkun* of the *Nefesh* is therefore achieved through the refinement of our physical deeds. When we use our bodies to perform a commandment, to do an act of charity, or to resist a physical temptation, we are purifying and elevating this level of our soul. Left to its own devices, the *Nefesh* is drawn to simple, material gratification, but when guided by the higher levels of the soul, it can become a powerful instrument for holiness in the material world.

Above the *Nefesh* resides the **Ruach**, which translates as "spirit" or "wind." This is the emotional soul, the seat of our personality. The *Ruach* is the source of the full spectrum of human feeling: love and fear, joy and sorrow, compassion and anger. It is the heart, not the mind or the body. Its consciousness is relational, concerned with the self in connection to others. It is the origin of our speech, which is emotion expressed as sound. The *Ruach* corresponds directly to the world of **Yetzirah**, the World of Formation, which is the realm of the emotions and the angels. Just as *Yetzirah* gives feeling and form to the intellectual blueprints of the world above it, our *Ruach* clothes our thoughts and instincts in emotion. The *tikkun* of the *Ruach* involves the purification of our character traits (*middot*). It is the difficult and essential work of transforming envy into appreciation, anger into resolve, and fear into reverence.

The highest of these three primary levels is the **Neshamah**, which translates as "breath," evoking the divine breath that God breathed into Adam. This is the intellectual soul, the higher mind. The *Neshamah* is the source of our capacity for abstract thought, contemplation, and intuition. It is the part of us that comprehends concepts, seeks meaning, and yearns for connection with the divine. It is not the "brain," which is a physical organ, but the pure consciousness that can grasp truth. The *Neshamah* is rooted in the world of **Beriah**, the World of Creation, the realm of the Divine Throne and pure intellect. The *tikkun* of the *Neshamah* is achieved through study, prayer, and meditation—practices that allow it to disengage from the noise of the lower levels and cleave to divine wisdom.

These three levels form an interactive system. A healthy spiritual life is one where the luminous understanding of the *Neshamah* guides and informs the emotions of the *Ruach*, which in turn directs the actions of the *Nefesh* in the physical world. A state of inner brokenness occurs when this hierarchy is inverted—when the raw physical urges of the *Nefesh* dictate the emotions of the *Ruach*, which then rationalizes its choices through the intellect of the *Neshamah*.

Beyond these, Luria taught of two even higher, transcendent levels of the soul that are generally beyond our conscious grasp but can be touched in moments of supreme spiritual ecstasy.

They are the **Chayah** ("Living Essence"), which corresponds to the world of *Atzilut* and to what is known as the divine blueprint of *Adam Kadmon*, and the **Yechidah** ("Unique Essence"), which is a spark of *Ein Sof* itself. Our mission in this life is to so purify our *Nefesh, Ruach,* and *Neshamah* that they become a clear channel, a holy vessel, for the infinite light of these higher dimensions to shine through us and into the world.

The Five Worlds and the Chain of Descent

After the cosmic cataclysm of the Shattering, creation could not be left in a state of utter chaos. The divine sparks had fallen, and the shards of the broken vessels formed the raw material of a lower reality. For the process of *Tikkun* to be possible, a new, more stable and complex structure was needed. A map of reality had to be drawn, a spiritual architecture that could house the great project of repair. This new, rectified order is conceived in the form of a cosmic anthropos, *Adam Kadmon* or "Primordial Man." This is not a physical being, but the metaphysical blueprint for all subsequent creation, a perfected configuration of the divine powers (*Sefirot*) that could withstand the flow of divine light. From this supernal template, reality unfolds downwards in a "Chain of Descent," a *Seder Hishtalshelut*, creating a series of layered worlds.

This Chain of Descent is the spiritual map of the universe. It explains how the singular, infinite reality of *Ein Sof* becomes the diverse, finite, and physical world we experience. Luria teaches that there are five primary worlds, each one a step further removed from the divine source, each one a realm of greater concealment and materiality. These are not separate physical locations like planets in a solar system; they are concentric dimensions of consciousness and being that interpenetrate and coexist, from the highest spiritual plane down to our own physical existence. Understanding this map is crucial, for it is the territory our souls must navigate on their journey of *tikkun*.

The five worlds are:

1. *Adam Kadmon* **(Primordial Man):**

   This is the highest and first manifestation after the *Tzimtzum*. It is the world of pure, unadulterated divine will and potential, the very thought of creation in the mind of God. It acts as the "buffer" and the interface between the infinite light of *Ein Sof* and all the worlds that will emerge from it. It is the realm of pure *Keter*, the Divine Crown, and the blueprint for everything that follows.

2. *Atzilut* **(World of Emanation):**

   Emanating from the "eyes, ears, nose, and mouth" of *Adam Kadmon*, *Atzilut* is the world of the pure *Sefirot*. Here, the divine attributes exist in a state of perfect unity and proximity to their source. There is no sense of separation between the emanator and the emanated. *Atzilut* is so close to the divine that it is considered to be one with it. It is the world of pure being, the realm of the Godhead as it can be related to. In this world, there are no *kelippot*, no shards, only pure light. It is the archetypal reality to which all the fallen sparks yearn to return.

3. ***Beriah* (World of Creation):**

Below *Atzilut*, across a "veil" that separates the purely divine from the created, lies the World of Creation. Here, for the first time, a sense of separateness arises. This is the world of the Divine Throne, the realm of the highest archangels, and the plane of pure intellect and thought. It is where the archetypal ideas from *Atzilut* are given their first distinct form as pure concepts. If *Atzilut* is the world of "being," *Beriah* is the world of "thinking." It is here that creation *ex nihilo*—"something from nothing"—truly occurs.

4. ***Yetzirah* (World of Formation):**

Descending further, we enter the World of Formation. This is the primary domain of the emotions and the realm of the vast majority of angels. The pure, intellectual blueprints of *Beriah* are now clothed in feeling and specific form. If *Beriah* is the architect's blueprint, *Yetzirah* is the vibrant, colorful rendering. It is a world of flowing emotion, sound, and archetypal imagery. It is the world of "feeling" and "speaking," the dimension that gives shape and passion to the thoughts from the world above.

5. *Asiyah* **(World of Action):**

This is the lowest and final world in the chain, the world of doing. *Asiyah* itself has two aspects: a spiritual dimension and a physical one. Its spiritual aspect is the immediate plane above our own, where the forms from *Yetzirah* are finalized and ready for manifestation. Its physical aspect *is* our material universe. This is the realm of maximum concealment of the divine light, where the holy sparks are most deeply embedded within the coarse shards of the *kelippot*. It is the world of "doing," the arena of action, and the primary stage for the human work of *tikkun*.

Navigating these worlds is the secret purpose of the soul's journey. Our souls are rooted in the higher worlds but are sent down into *Asiyah* on a mission. Our task is to perform physical actions

(*Asiyah*) infused with holy emotion (*Yetzirah*) and guided by sacred intellect (*Beriah*), all with the intention of connecting back to the divine unity of *Atzilut*. A single act of *tikkun* is a multi-dimensional event. The physical act happens here, in our world, but its effects reverberate all the way up the chain, bringing light and healing to all levels of being. Prayer, meditation, and ethical living are not just behaviors; they are techniques for traversing and unifying these worlds, building a ladder from our fragmented reality back to the divine source.

The Soul and Reincarnation (Gilgulim)

The great cosmic drama of Shattering and Repair is not merely an external event that happened long ago. It is an ongoing process that is mirrored in the deepest recesses of the human soul. Just as the primordial vessels broke apart, the original, holistic soul of humanity—*Adam HaRishon*, the first man—also fragmented. For Isaac Luria, the soul is not a simple, monolithic entity that inhabits a body. It is a complex, multi-layered, and dynamic being with its own history, its own wounds, and its own sacred mission of *tikkun*. To understand our place in the universe, we must first understand the Ari's revolutionary vision of the soul's journey through time, the doctrine of *Gilgulim*, or reincarnation.

Luria's first radical insight was to move beyond the idea of a single, individual soul. He taught that humanity is composed of a finite number of great "soul roots," or *shoresh neshama*. Imagine a vast, luminous tree in the higher worlds. Each major branch of this tree is a soul root, and every individual soul on earth is like a leaf or a twig growing from that branch. Therefore, we are not isolated spiritual beings; we are part of a larger spiritual family, connected at our root to many other souls. This explains the inexplicable bonds and affinities we feel with certain people—they may be sparks from the same primordial root. Furthermore, an individual person is rarely comprised of just one simple soul-spark. More often, a person is a composite being, containing sparks from different roots, or even "impregnations" (*ibbur*) of other soul-energies, both positive and negative, that attach themselves to a person to help or hinder their spiritual work. This complex vision of the soul accounts for the multifaceted, often contradictory nature of our own inner lives.

With this complex soul as the protagonist, the doctrine of *Gilgulim* becomes the plot. The Hebrew word *gilgul* means "cycle" or "transmigration." For Luria, reincarnation is not simply a system of cosmic reward and punishment, nor is it an endless, meaningless cycle. It is the core mechanism of *Tikkun Olam*. Souls are sent back into the physical world (*Asiyah*) for one primary reason: they have a mission to complete. The soul is a soldier for God, sent down to the battlefield of material existence on a specific assignment. That assignment is its personal *tikkun*.

This personal *tikkun* is breathtakingly specific. A soul may be reborn because in a previous life it transgressed a particular commandment, and it must now be placed in a situation where it can rectify that failure. More profoundly, a soul is sent to a particular time, place, and family because there are specific, scattered sparks of holiness (*nitzotzot*) that only *that* soul has the ability to redeem. Your unique combination of talents, challenges, and life circumstances is not an accident. It is the precise toolkit and curriculum designed for your soul's rectification work. The Ari was said to have the spiritual vision to look at a person's forehead and read their entire history of *gilgulim*, identifying the source of their soul, the mistakes of their past lives, and the specific tasks required of them in this one.

This perspective imbues every human life with an immense and sacred purpose. The frustrating, repetitive challenges you face may be the very curriculum your soul needs to master to complete its repair. The people who drive you to distraction may be souls you are connected to from past lives, brought together again to finally resolve an ancient conflict and, in doing so, release a trapped spark of light. The unexplainable longing you feel for a certain place, a certain field of knowledge, or a certain type of work may be the echo of your soul's mission calling to you. In the Lurianic view, there are no insignificant lives. The humblest person, by performing their unique *tikkun* with conscious intention (*kavvanah*), is doing a work of cosmic importance.

This lens of reincarnation provides a powerful framework for understanding the deepest questions of human experience.

- **Suffering:** Why do we suffer? From the perspective of *gilgulim*, suffering is never meaningless. It can be a process of purification, the cleansing of a stain from a past life. It can also be the very friction necessary to crack open the *kelippah*, the shard, that holds a precious spark captive. The struggle itself is part of the work.

- **Dreams:** The Ari taught that during sleep, the soul ascends to the higher worlds, particularly the World of Formation (*Yetzirah*). Dreams are therefore not random firings of the brain but can be genuine spiritual experiences. They can offer glimpses into past lives, warnings about future challenges, and guidance for one's current *tikkun*.

- **Human Connections:** The people in our lives are not random assortments. Our family, our friends, and even our enemies are often members of our "soul group," souls we have traveled with across many lifetimes. We come together to help one another, to challenge one another, and to complete a collective *tikkun* that we could not achieve alone.

The doctrine of *Gilgulim* is ultimately a message of profound hope and radical responsibility. It tells us that our lives are not a brief, meaningless flash of existence, but a single, crucial chapter in the soul's epic journey of return. We have been here before, and we will be here again, until the great work of repair is finally complete. Our personal healing is cosmic healing; our individual journey of rectification is an indispensable part of reuniting the shattered universe with its infinite source.

The Tree of Life in Lurianic Perspective

The Tree of Life, the diagram of the ten *Sefirot*, is the most iconic symbol of Kabbalah. For centuries before Isaac Luria, it was understood primarily as a static map, a hierarchical ladder illustrating the orderly descent of divine energy from the infinite source down into the created world. It was a sublime and logical diagram of divine attributes, a blueprint of cosmic perfection. But when the Ari gazed upon this ancient symbol, he saw something entirely different. He saw not a static chart, but a living, breathing, dynamic organism. He saw a cosmic drama of tension, flow, crisis, and resolution. Luria did not discard the Tree of Life; he set it in motion, transforming it from a map of divine states into the very engine of the cosmic process of Shattering and Repair.

In the Lurianic vision, the *Sefirot* are not simply passive containers or stable attributes. They are active, interacting forces, centers of immense spiritual energy that are constantly in relationship with one another. To capture this dynamic quality, Luria introduced a revolutionary concept: the *Partzufim*, or "Divine Faces" (or Personas). He taught that after the catastrophe of the Shattering of the Vessels, the *Sefirot* did not simply reform. They reconfigured themselves into complex, composite personalities, much like different organs and limbs come together to form a complete human body.

Instead of ten isolated points, the *Sefirot* now arranged themselves into five primary *Partzufim*:

1. ***Arikh Anpin* (The Long Face/The Infinitely Patient One):**

   Primarily associated with the *sefirah* of *Keter* (Crown), this is the supernal divine will, the source of all compassion and pleasure that flows into creation.

2. ***Abba* (The Father):**

   A configuration that is centered around the *sefirah* of *Chokhmah* (Wisdom). *Abba* re presents the primordial, undifferentiated spark of insight, the first flash of creative intellect.

3. ***Imma* (The Mother):**

   A configuration that is centered around *Binah* (Understanding). *Imma* take s the seed-like flash of *Abba* and gestates it in her "womb," giving it breadth, depth, and structure, developing it into a fully articulated thought.

4. **Zeir Anpin (The Small Face/The Impatient One):**

This is the most complex *Partzuf*. It is a composite of the six central *Sefirot* (*Chesed, Gevurah, Tiferet, Netzach, Hod, Yesod*). *Zeir Anpin* represents the masculine divine archetype, the "Son," who channels the intellectual energy of *Abba* and *Imma* into the lower worlds. He is the active, emotional principle in the Godhead, analogous to the sun that shines its light upon the world.

5. **Nukva (The Female):**

A configuration that is centered on the lowest *sefirah*, *Malkhut* (Kingdom), this is the feminine divine archetype, the "Daughter," often identified with the *Shekhinah* (also known as the Divine Presence). *Nukva* has no light of her own; her role is to receive the light from *Zeir Anpin* and manifest it in creation, just as the moon receives and reflects the light of the sun. Our physical world, *Asiyah*, is the manifestation of *Nukva*.

This drama of the *Partzufim* is the story of the universe. The state of exile and brokenness is a state where the flow of light between these Divine

Faces is impaired. Specifically, it is a state where the union between *Zeir Anpin* (the Son) and *Nukva* (the Daughter) is incomplete. The goal of *Tikkun* is to facilitate their sacred union, the *Yichud*, which allows divine energy to flow harmoniously through all of creation, restoring cosmic balance. Our actions, thoughts, and intentions on earth directly affect the relationships between these supernal personalities.

This dynamic interplay is structured around the three columns of the Tree of Life. The Right column, headed by *Chokhmah*, is the pillar of expansion, mercy, and giving (*Chesed*). The Left column, headed by *Binah*, is the pillar of restriction, judgment, and receiving (*Gevurah*). The Middle column, headed by *Keter* and *Tiferet*, is the pillar of balance and synthesis. Before the Shattering, the vessels of the Left column, representing severe Judgment, were too strong and isolated, unable to receive the expansive light from the Right. This imbalance precipitated the catastrophe. The work of *Tikkun* is therefore the work of weaving together the energies of the Right and Left, bringing mercy to bear on judgment, and strengthening the Middle path of balance. Every ethical choice we make is a microcosm of this cosmic balancing act. Choosing compassion over anger, generosity over selfishness, is an act that strengthens the Middle column, not just within ourselves, but within the divine architecture itself.

For Luria, the Tree of Life is not a diagram to be studied, but a dynamic system to be engaged with. It is the blueprint for both God and the human soul, which is created in its image. The drama of the divine light—its flow, its blockages, its union, its exile—is mirrored in our own psychological and spiritual lives. By understanding the interactions between the *Sefirot* and the drama of the *Partzufim*, we gain insight into the hidden forces that shape our reality and learn how to consciously participate in the great dance of divine light and cosmic restoration.

The Other Side: Kelippot and the Anatomy of Evil

In a cosmos defined by the sacred task of *tikkun*, of gathering and elevating light, there must exist an opposing force—a metaphysical gravity that holds the sparks down, a spiritual entropy that works to keep the universe fragmented. Isaac Luria provides a detailed and chilling anatomy of this opposition. This is not a simple dualism of a "good God" versus a "devil." It is a far more sophisticated vision of a shadow system that exists as a parasitic consequence of the *Shevirah*, the Shattering of the Vessels. This is the realm of the **Kelippot** (the Shells or Husks), which form a coherent, anti-holy structure known as the **Sitra Achra**, Aramaic for "The Other Side."

The *Kelippot* are more than just the inert shards of the broken vessels. They are active, dynamic forces of concealment. Think of them as layers of spiritual plaque that build up around the holy sparks, obscuring their light and drawing sustenance from them. They are not a source of being themselves; they are parasites on the divine energy they imprison. Their entire nature is to take, to absorb, and to separate. While the side of Holiness (*Kedushah*) is defined by giving, connection, and revelation, the *Sitra Achra* is defined by receiving for the self alone, by isolation, and by concealment. It is the cosmic government of ego.

Luria provides a precise taxonomy of this shadow realm. He teaches that there are two primary categories of *kelippot*. First, there are **three completely impure *kelippot*.** These are opaque, impenetrable shells, representing absolute spiritual darkness. They are the metaphysical roots of what we would call pure evil—cruelty for its own sake, utter godlessness, and actions that are irredeemable. They have no connection to holiness and are destined to be annihilated in the final *tikkun*.

Far more relevant to our daily human experience is the fourth and most subtle shell: ***Kelippat Nogah***, the "Glowing Shell." *Nogah* is a translucent husk. It is not purely dark; rather, it is an ambiguous mixture of good and evil, light and shadow. The vast majority of our worldly reality exists within this *Kelippat Nogah*. A piece of fruit, money, a worldly ambition, a physical desire—all these things exist within *Nogah*. They are not inherently holy or unholy; their spiritual destiny depends entirely on our intention. If one eats the fruit with a blessing and the intention to gain strength for spiritual service, the spark of life-force within the fruit is elevated to the side of

Holiness, and the shell falls away. If one eats it gluttonously, the spark is degraded and dragged further down into the realm of the impure *kelippot*. *Kelippat Nogah* is the battlefield of human choice.

This leads to a terrifying conclusion: our actions directly nourish one side or the other. When a person sins—acts with selfishness, cruelty, or idolatrous desire (which includes treating any finite thing as an ultimate source of happiness)— they are taking a spark of divine energy that animates them and actively channeling it to the *Sitra Achra*. A sin is a metaphysical transaction that strengthens the prisons holding all other sparks captive. It feeds the forces of concealment and thickens the veil that separates the world from God. The *Sitra Achra* has no life of its own; it survives only on the divine energy we divert to it through our negative choices.

The mystic, therefore, is a warrior in a constant, cosmic battle. This is not a battle against an external enemy, but against the forces of concealment that operate both outside and inside the human heart. The spiritual dangers are real. Giving in to pride, despair, or sensual indulgence for its own sake strengthens the *kelippot* around one's own soul, making it harder to hear the voice of the *Neshamah*. This is the deep struggle of the

Lurianic path: to live in a world governed by *Kelippat Nogah* and to consistently make the choices that rescue the light, starving the Other Side and bringing nourishment to the side of Holiness.

Divine Names and Sacred Intention

In the Lurianic universe, reality is not built from matter and energy, but from a substance far more potent: language. Specifically, it is built from the twenty-two letters of the Hebrew alphabet. For the Kabbalist, these letters are not mere symbols for phonetic sounds. They are the primordial spiritual forces, the raw elements, the very DNA of creation. The ancient mystical text, *Sefer Yetzirah* ("The Book of Formation"), states that God created the world by "engraving" and combining these letters. Isaac Luria took this foundational idea and developed it into a practical, high-stakes technology of the soul. If the universe is made of letters, then combining them in the right way, with the right intention, can affect the very fabric of reality.

This is the basis for the Ari's complex meditative practices involving divine names. The Torah is filled with various names for God—Y-H-V-H, Elohim, Adonai, Shaddai, and so on. In Lurianic Kabbalah, these are not synonyms; they are distinct conduits for different types of divine energy, each corresponding to a specific *sefirah* or *partzuf* on the Tree of Life. For instance, the name associated with *Chesed* (Mercy) is different from the one associated with *Gevurah* (Judgment). The true magic lies in the art of *yiḥudim* (unifications).

A *yiḥud* is a meditative practice where the Kabbalist visualizes the intertwining and unification of different divine names. By doing this, they are actively building a bridge between different divine forces, helping to heal a rupture in the supernal worlds. For example, by meditating on the unification of a name for *Zeir Anpin* (the divine "Son") and a name for *Nukva* (the divine "Daughter"), the mystic actively participates in and facilitates their sacred union, which is the ultimate goal of *tikkun*.

This is a form of theurgy—the belief that human ritual and mental activity can influence the divine realms. It is a spirituality of immense empowerment and immense responsibility. The mystic is not just praying *to* God; they are working *on* the very structure of the Godhead, helping to mend its internal relationships and restore the harmonious flow of light throughout the cosmos.

This high-level meditative work found its most accessible and widespread application in the practice of *kavvanot* (intentions). While the intricate art of *yiḥudim* was reserved for the most advanced adepts, the principle of *kavvanah* could be applied by any devoted individual. As we have seen, *kavvanah* is the directing of consciousness, the focused intention that gives an action its spiritual power. For Luria, this was not a vague feeling of sincerity. He developed a system of highly specific *kavvanot* to be used during prayer and the performance of religious commandments (*mitzvot*).

When a Lurianic mystic puts on *tefillin* (phylacteries), they are not just performing a ritual act. In their mind, they are visualizing the flow of light from the higher intellect (*Chokhmah* and *Binah*) down into the emotional center (*Zeir Anpin*), binding the divine mind to the divine heart. When they say the *Shema* prayer ("Hear, O Israel, the Lord is our God, the Lord is One"), they are not just declaring monotheism. With the proper *kavvanot*, they are performing a complex sequence of *yiḥudim*, unifying the divine masculine and feminine aspects, raising the fallen sparks, and creating a shield of spiritual protection around themselves for the day. Every word of the standard liturgy became a trigger for a specific visualization and mystical intention. Prayer was transformed from a petitionary dialogue into a theurgical operation, a spiritual "mission control" where the person at prayer becomes a conscious engineer of cosmic energies.

This is *tikkun* through sound, thought, and alignment. The vibrations of the sacred words, amplified by the laser-focus of human consciousness, become the tools for cosmic repair. The Lurianic Kabbalist lives in a world humming with power and potential. The name of God is not just a word to be revered, but a formula to be used. The letters of the alphabet are not just for writing books, but for rewriting reality. This profound belief in the creative power of human consciousness, focused through the lens of sacred language and divine names, is one of the Ari's most enduring and potent legacies. It insists that we are not merely creatures in the world, but co-creators of its spiritual state, armed with the power of our own minds to heal the great schism that began at the dawn of time.

The Feminine Presence and the Shabbat Bride

In the cosmic drama of Isaac Luria, no figure is more central, poignant, and vital than the *Shekhinah*—the feminine face of God. In earlier Kabbalah, the *Shekhinah* was identified with the lowest *sefirah*, *Malkhut* (Kingdom), representing the divine presence as it manifests within the created world. She was the point of contact between the transcendent Godhead and the immanent world. But in the Ari's dynamic and dramatic vision, she takes on a far more active and tragic role. The *Shekhinah* is not simply the presence of God in the world; she is the presence of God *in exile*.

When the Primordial Vessels shattered, it was *Malkhut*, the final vessel, that broke most completely and fell the furthest. The *Shekhinah* is therefore inextricably linked with the fate of the scattered sparks of light. She is the divine mother goose whose ducklings have been lost and scattered across the world. Her cosmic reality is one of sorrow and longing. She wanders through the broken world, grieving for her lost children—the sparks—and yearning for reunion with her masculine counterpart, *Zeir Anpin* (the divine "Son" or "King"). The exile of the Jewish people from their land is, in the Lurianic imagination, a physical reflection of this much deeper, metaphysical exile. The suffering of the world is the suffering of the *Shekhinah*. She is the Queen whose kingdom has been shattered, the mother who has been separated from her beloved.

The entire project of *Tikkun Olam* can therefore be understood as the restoration of the divine feminine. Every spark that is raised from its captivity in the shards of the *kelippot* is one of her lost children being returned to her. Every act of *tikkun* helps to rebuild her shattered vessel of *Malkhut*. The ultimate goal of cosmic repair is the *Yichud*, the sacred union or marriage, between the *Shekhinah* (*Nukva*, the Female) and *Zeir Anpin* (the divine King). When this union is complete, the flow of divine grace is restored to all worlds, and the exile comes to an end. Our spiritual work is, in essence, the work of cosmic matchmaking—of healing the rift between the masculine and feminine aspects of God, thereby healing all of creation.

This profound focus on the feminine divine found its most beautiful and enduring expression in the Lurianic innovations to the liturgy of Shabbat, the Sabbath. For the Ari and his circle of mystics in Safed, Shabbat was not merely a day of rest. It was a weekly taste of the World to Come, a 25-hour period where the cosmic union between the divine King and Queen could be most fully realized. The rituals of Friday night were re-imagined as a ceremony to welcome and enthrone a celestial guest: the Shabbat Queen, who is an embodiment of the *Shekhinah* herself.

Luria and his disciples would dress in white garments and walk out into the fields of Safed as the sun began to set on Friday afternoon. Facing the west, they would greet the incoming Sabbath not just as a period of time, but as a royal personage, the mystical Bride. It was in this context that one of Luria's students, Rabbi Shlomo Alkabetz, composed the hauntingly beautiful hymn, *Lekha Dodi* ("Come, My Beloved"), which is now a centerpiece of Friday night services in every synagogue in the world. The poem is a love song, operating on multiple levels: it is the Jewish people calling to their beloved God, but at its deepest mystical level, it is the divine King (*Zeir Anpin*) calling out to his beloved Bride, the *Shekhinah*, inviting her to their sacred union. Singing this hymn becomes a way for the community to actively participate in and facilitate this supernal wedding.

The entire Friday night meal was likewise transformed into a reflection of this mystical marriage. The two candles lit on the table represent the two partners. The two loaves of *challah* bread symbolize their embrace. The meal itself, conducted with joy and song, provides the nurturing, terrestrial energy needed to sustain the supernal union. For the Ari, Shabbat became the great weekly opportunity for *tikkun*. It was the time when the heavens were most open, when the Queen was closest to her King, and when human actions had the most potent effect on the spiritual worlds. Through these rituals, Luria gave the Jewish people a living, weekly practice for healing the divine feminine, mending the cosmos, and experiencing the profound love and harmony that is the ultimate goal of all creation.

Living the Tikkun: Rituals for Daily Life

The Lurianic system, for all its towering metaphysical complexity, is not meant to be a theoretical philosophy. It is an operational manual for living a life of cosmic significance. The Ari and his disciples in Safed were not armchair mystics; they were spiritual technicians who infused every moment of their day with the conscious work of *tikkun*. They developed and popularized a host of practices that transformed mundane, everyday actions into potent rituals of world-repair. This chapter explores some of these key practices, revealing how the grand drama of Shattering and Repair can be engaged with from the kitchen table to the midnight vigil.

Perhaps the most fundamental practice involves **food and blessings**. For Luria, eating is never a neutral act. Every piece of food, every drop of water, contains holy sparks of divine life force (*nitzotzot*) trapped within a shell (*kelippah*) of materiality. The purpose of eating is to perform a spiritual separation. When a person recites the proper blessing (*bracha*) over food with focused intention (*kavvanah*), they act as a spiritual catalyst. The sacred words, powered by human consciousness, separate the spark from its shell. The body is nourished by the physical aspect (the shell), while the soul elevates the spiritual essence (the spark), returning it to its divine source. To eat mindlessly, without a blessing, is to miss the opportunity entirely. The spark remains imprisoned, and the person merely gratifies their physical drive, an act that can even strengthen the *kelippah*. The dinner table thus becomes an altar, and every meal a sacred operation.

One of the most powerful and distinctive Lurianic rituals is the ***Tikkun Chatzot***, the "Midnight Rectification." Luria taught that midnight is a time of cosmic transition, when the divine attribute of Judgment (*Gevurah*) is most potent in the world. It is a moment of great spiritual severity, but also great potential. He instructed his disciples to rise from their sleep at this hour, sit on the floor in mourning, and recite a series of psalms and lamentations. The primary focus of this vigil is to grieve for the destruction of the Temple in Jerusalem, but on a mystical level, it is an act of profound empathy with the divine. The mystic mourns for the exile of the *Shekhinah* and the shattered state of the cosmos. By consciously sharing in God's sorrow, they bring comfort to the Divine Presence and sweeten the harsh energies of Judgment with their tears and prayers, preparing the world for the new flow of Mercy (*Chesed*) that will come with the dawn.

Purification of the self was also central. The Ari placed immense importance on **mystical immersion, or** *tevilah,* in a natural spring or a ritual bath (*mikvah*). This was not about hygiene. For Luria, immersing in "living water" was a symbolic return to the protective, purifying womb of *Imma Ila'ah,* the Supernal Mother (the *partzuf* of *Binah*). This act could wash away the spiritual residue of the *kelippot* that clings to a person after a negative interaction, a bad dream, or a moral failing. Luria himself would immerse daily, believing it was essential for clearing the spiritual senses to perceive the hidden realities of the world.

The Ari's famous walks in the fields were also a form of ritual.

He practiced *yichudim* **(unifications) in nature,** meditating on the unification of divine names to aid the souls he could perceive were reincarnated in trees, rocks, and springs. This practice cultivates an awareness of the entire natural world as being alive with consciousness and filled with sparks crying out for redemption. It transforms a simple walk in the woods into a mission of spiritual rescue.

From the moment of waking—reciting the *Modeh Ani* prayer to consciously thank God for returning the soul—to the moment of sleep—reciting the bedtime *Shema* to entrust one's soul to the divine for protection—the Lurianic path sanctifies the entire 24-hour cycle. It is a path of relentless consciousness, a commitment to seeing every moment as an opportunity. It is not a spirituality for one day a week, but an operating system for a life dedicated, breath by breath, to the sacred, urgent, and hopeful work of *Tikkun Olam*.

The Mystical Meaning of Exile and Redemption

The concepts of exile (*galut*) and redemption (*geulah*) are central to Jewish thought, traditionally understood through a historical lens: the exile from the Land of Israel and the messianic hope for a future return. Isaac Luria, looking through his Kabbalistic lens, profoundly deepened and universalized these concepts. For the Ari, exile is not primarily a political or geographical condition; it is the fundamental metaphysical state of the universe. The world itself is in exile from its divine source. The *Shekhinah* is in exile from her beloved. The sparks of light are in exile, trapped in their shells. Our souls are in exile from their roots. The historical displacement of the Jewish people is merely the most tangible, human-level symptom of this all-pervasive cosmic rupture.

This perspective answers the agonizing question, "Why is the world so broken?" in a startlingly original way. The world is broken not because of God's anger or humanity's sin, but because it was born from a necessary and purposeful catastrophe. The Shattering of the Vessels was not a divine mistake. Luria offers a stunning paradox: the cosmic break was essential to allow for free will, moral struggle, and the possibility of *tikkun*. If the world had been created in a state of seamless perfection, there would be no room for human striving. Our choices would have no consequence. We would be puppets in a perfect, but static, divine play.

The Shattering created a world of moral ambiguity, of hidden holiness and manifest darkness. It created a reality where good and evil are mixed, where the light is concealed, and where choices matter. This brokenness is precisely what gives our lives meaning. It creates the conditions for us to become what Luria believed was our destiny: co-creators with God. The exile of the sparks into the realm of the *kelippot* was a deliberate act of divine investment. God "invested" parts of Himself into the lowest realms of being so that humanity, through its own free-willed actions, could find this divine capital, refine it, and return it with "interest," thereby raising creation to a level even higher than its original potential. Exile, therefore, is not a punishment; it is a vocation.

If exile is the metaphysical condition of the cosmos, then what is redemption? For Luria, redemption is not a single, future event where a messiah will suddenly appear and fix the world. Rather, it is a gradual, cumulative *process* that is happening right now, powered by the collective spiritual work of humanity throughout history. The Ari's messianic vision is profoundly process-oriented. He taught that every single act of *tikkun*, no matter how small, has a real, quantifiable effect. Every spark that is elevated brings the final redemption one step closer.

Imagine a gigantic, cosmic puzzle with billions of pieces. The final picture is the redeemed world. Every time a person performs a commandment with *kavvanah*, or resists a negative impulse, or acts with selfless kindness, they find one of the missing puzzle pieces and click it into place. The messiah cannot come until a critical mass of this repair work has been completed by humanity. We are not waiting for redemption; we are building it. The messianic age is not something that happens *to* us; it is something that emerges *from* us.

This culminates in the idea that inner awakening is the catalyst for universal redemption. The great work of *tikkun* is not just about external rituals; it is about the purification and elevation of one's own consciousness. The macrocosm (the universe) and the microcosm (the human being) are reflections of each other. By healing the fragmentation within our own souls, by integrating the conflicting parts of our own psyche, and by aligning our personal will with the divine will, we are simultaneously healing the fragmentation in the supernal worlds.

The Ari's eschatology—his vision of the end times—is therefore not a passive doctrine of hope, but an urgent call to action. It is a message of profound optimism, grounded in radical responsibility. The ultimate fate of the universe rests on our shoulders. The redemption of the world depends on the accumulation of small, sacred acts performed by ordinary people in their daily lives. Luria provides a vision where history has a purpose, where human life has a mission, and where the brokenness of our world is not a sign of despair, but the very ground of our greatest hope.

The Messianic Process: Building Redemption, Spark by Spark

In most religious traditions, the coming of a Messiah is imagined as a singular, dramatic event—a divine intervention where a chosen figure arrives to redeem a fallen world. Isaac Luria, in one of his most profound reinterpretations, transformed this passive hope into an active, urgent spiritual project. For the Ari, redemption (*geulah*) is not an event we wait for; it is a **process we build**. The messianic age is not a gift to be handed down from heaven; it is a structure being assembled on earth, piece by piece, spark by spark, by the cumulative spiritual labor of every soul throughout history.

Luria taught that the final redemption is contingent upon the completion of *Tikkun Olam*. Every time a person elevates a fallen spark of holiness through a conscious, sacred act, they are laying another brick in the edifice of the messianic era. Redemption is the sum total of all the *tikkunim* (repairs) ever performed. This recasts the messiah not as a savior who does the work for us, but as the master builder who arrives to install the capstone on a temple that we ourselves have been building for millennia. We are not waiting for the messiah; the messiah is waiting for us to finish our work.

This leads to a deeper understanding of the messianic figure itself. Luria speaks of the **collective soul of the Messiah**. This is not just one individual soul, but a vast, composite soul comprised of the highest and purest sparks from all the most righteous souls who have ever lived. Throughout history, these individuals— the *tzaddikim* or "righteous ones"—serve as the primary agents of redemption. A *tzaddik* is a spiritual powerhouse, a soul so pure that their actions have immense cosmic leverage. A single prayer or act of self-sacrifice by a *tzaddik* can achieve a level of *tikkun* that might require the work of thousands of ordinary people. They are the chief engineers of the redemptive process, consciously working to gather and elevate sparks on a massive scale, thereby accelerating the timetable for the final *geulah*. The soul of the final messianic king will be the ultimate vessel, the one that finally incorporates and manifests the completed state of this collective messianic soul.

This Lurianic perspective elegantly addresses the question: **Is the Messiah a person or an era of consciousness?** The answer is that it is both, inextricably linked. The process of *tikkun* is the process of gradually building a new global consciousness—an era where the divine light is no longer concealed, where the presence of God is manifest and obvious to all. The world becomes transparent to its divine source. This *era* is the true goal. The messianic *person* is the final agent who embodies this new consciousness so completely that his presence tips the scales, inaugurating the era for the entire world. He is the first citizen of the completed world, the one whose personal *tikkun* is so perfect that it completes the *tikkun* of all creation.

What, then, is the **Lurianic vision of the final state of the world?** It is not merely a return to a primordial, untested Garden of Eden. It is an elevation to a state far superior to the one that existed before the Shattering. The process of being broken, scattered, and painstakingly reassembled creates a reality that is infinitely more complex, resilient, and conscious than the original. In the messianic age, the *kelippot* will be fully stripped away or transformed into vessels of holiness. The flow between the *partzufim* will be perfected in a permanent, loving union. The distinction between the physical and spiritual will dissolve, and the entire universe will radiate with the manifest light of *Ein Sof*. It is the ultimate fulfillment of the divine plan, a world made holy not by divine fiat from above, but by the sacred, difficult, and heroic labor of humanity from below.

Tzimtzum as Spiritual Practice

The grand cosmic principles of Lurianic Kabbalah are not meant to remain in the celestial realms of metaphysical speculation. Their true power is realized when they are brought down to earth and applied as practical guides for living a more conscious and ethical life. Of all the Ari's foundational concepts, it is *Tzimtzum*, the primordial contraction of divine light, that offers the most immediate and profound model for spiritual practice. If the very first act of the Infinite was an act of self-limitation to create space for another to exist, then this becomes the blueprint for our most sacred human interactions.

At its core, practicing *tzimtzum* means consciously making space. In a world that encourages constant self-expression, self-promotion, and the expansion of the ego, the spiritual path of *tzimtzum* is a radical counter-current. It is the art of holy withdrawal. It is the recognition that sometimes the most powerful, creative, and loving thing we can do is to become smaller, quieter, and less present, so that something or someone else can emerge into the space we have vacated. This practice can transform our relationships, our inner life, and our fundamental orientation to the world.

The most direct application is found in the ethics of dialogue and relationship. How often in a conversation are we truly listening, versus simply waiting for our turn to speak? How often is our "listening" just an exercise in formulating our own rebuttal, our own story, our own piece of advice? To practice *tzimtzum* in conversation is to contract one's own ego, to pull back the relentless forward-drive of one's own agenda, thoughts, and opinions. It is to create a genuine, receptive emptiness in which the other person can feel safe enough to truly unfold. It means listening not just to their words, but to the silence between them, to the emotion behind them. This act of making space for the other to be fully seen and heard is a profound act of love and respect. It is a microcosm of the divine act of creation. In that moment, you are creating a world for another person. This applies not only to conversations but to all relationships—with a partner, a child, or a friend—where allowing them the space to be themselves, without the oppressive weight of our expectations, is the greatest gift we can offer.

This principle extends inward as a powerful tool for mindfulness and self-awareness. The human mind is a noisy place, constantly filled with the chatter of the ego—its fears, its desires, its judgments, its endless narratives. This inner noise can be so loud that it drowns out the more subtle and authentic whispers of the soul. Practicing *tzimtzum* in mindfulness is the act of intentionally withdrawing energy from the clamor of the ego. It is not about fighting the thoughts or suppressing them, but about gently pulling back from them, creating an inner space of quiet observation.

As we contract our identification with the surface-level ego, we create a sacred void within. It is in this inner stillness that deeper truths can arise. The voice of intuition, the quiet knowing of the heart, the guidance of the soul—these can only be heard when we have made room for them. This inner contraction is the prerequisite for any genuine self-knowledge or connection to the divine. We must make space within ourselves to receive what is greater than ourselves.

Ultimately, the practice of *tzimtzum* cultivates the foundational virtue for all spiritual work: humility (*anavah* in Hebrew). In the Lurianic view, the ego's arrogance and insistence on taking up all the space is the root of the *kelippot*, the hard shells that trap the light. The ego says, "I am everything." Humility, born of *tzimtzum*, says, "I will make space for you." This is not a self-negating or passive humility, but a potent, generative one. It is the strength to be a container rather than just a projector. It is the wisdom to know that real power lies not in asserting the self, but in creating the conditions for life, truth, and love to flourish. By practicing the sacred art of contraction in our daily lives, we emulate the very first act of God and become partners in the ongoing work of creation.

Tikkun in a Fragmented World

Isaac Luria's call for *Tikkun Olam*—the Repair of the World—was born in a 16th-century context of ritual, prayer, and mystical meditation. Yet the power of his vision is so immense that it cannot be confined to the synagogue or the study hall. It breaks free, offering a profound and urgent framework for engaging with the challenges of our modern, fragmented world. The Ari's wisdom demands that we expand our understanding of *tikkun* beyond its original religious confines and see it as a call to sacred responsibility in every dimension of our lives. If divine sparks are truly scattered everywhere, then the work of repair must also be done everywhere.

This expanded vision invites us to find the hidden sparks in all aspects of contemporary life. Our work, our art, our relationships, and our civic engagement all become potential arenas for *tikkun*. A scientist working to cure a disease, a teacher patiently nurturing a student's mind, an artist creating a work of beauty that uplifts the human spirit, a therapist helping a client integrate the broken pieces of their psyche—all of these can be seen as potent acts of raising the sparks. The key, as always, is *kavvanah*, intention. When we approach our work not just as a job but as a sacred calling, as a way to bring more light, healing, or order into a small corner of the world, we transform our labor into a Lurianic spiritual practice.

In an age of ecological crisis, the Ari's cosmology provides a powerful foundation for what can be called sacred environmentalism. Our planet is not a dead resource to be exploited; it is a living entity, a vast tapestry of divine sparks embedded in physical forms. The pollution of our rivers, the destruction of our forests, and the poisoning of our atmosphere are, in Kabbalistic terms, a desecration. It is the act of thickening the *kelippot*, the shells, making it harder for the divine light within nature to shine. Conversely, acts of conservation, restoration, and sustainable living are powerful forms of *tikkun*. Planting a tree, cleaning a shoreline, or choosing a lifestyle that honors the earth's limits are not just ethical choices; they are acts of cosmic repair, helping to heal the shattered vessel of the living world.

Similarly, Lurianic thought can fuel a unique form of sacred activism. The injustices of our society—poverty, racism, oppression—are manifestations of the *Shevirah*, the Shattering. They are the social equivalent of the shards, systems of brokenness that trap and diminish the divine spark within human beings. Working to dismantle these unjust systems, to feed the hungry, to advocate for the marginalized, and to build communities based on compassion and equity is *tikkun* in its most visible and potent form. It is the work of reassembling the broken pieces of the human family. This activism is not fueled by anger and hatred for the "other," which only strengthens the *kelippot* of division. Rather, it is fueled by a deep, loving recognition of the divine spark in every person and a fierce commitment to liberating that spark from the external and internal shells that confine it.

Finally, the work of *tikkun* must be applied to our own inner worlds. We live in an age of anxiety, trauma, and psychological fragmentation. Healing our own personal traumas is not a selfish act; it is a form of cosmic repair. Every time we integrate a shadow aspect of our personality, heal a childhood wound, or overcome a destructive pattern, we are performing a *tikkun* on the microcosm of our own soul. This inner work is essential, for we can only mend the world to the extent that we are mended ourselves. An unhealed person trying to heal the world will often, unconsciously, project their own brokenness onto their work. By healing ourselves, we become clearer and more effective vessels for the work of healing others.

The enduring legacy of Isaac Luria is this call to radical, all-encompassing responsibility. He bequeathed to us a vision of a universe that is not static or distant, but is a dynamic, living organism that desperately needs our help. His teachings pull spirituality out of the abstract and place it squarely in the midst of our messy, beautiful, broken world. In every moment, in every choice, we are either reinforcing the fragmentation or we are participating in the sacred, hopeful, and urgent work of its repair.

The Blueprint and the Mystery

We began this journey with the most enduring of human questions: why is a world created by a good God so full of brokenness, and what is our role in it? Through the incandescent vision of Isaac Luria, we have explored one of the most daring and profound answers ever offered. The universe, in the Ari's telling, is not a finished product but a dynamic and perilous process. It is a cosmic story in three acts: a divine contraction to make space, a catastrophic shattering of the vessels that filled that space, and a sacred, ongoing project of human-led repair.

This is the Lurianic blueprint. It re-enchants the world, revealing the hidden metaphysical drama playing out behind the curtain of mundane reality. It tells us that the universe we inhabit is a mixture of sublime light and coarse shards, a battleground where exiled sparks of divinity yearn for liberation. It transforms our understanding of ourselves, casting us not as passive observers or fallen sinners, but as the indispensable ground crew for creation, the partners of God tasked with the monumental work of *Tikkun Olam*.

The Ari's wisdom gives context and meaning to our struggles. The psychological fragmentation we feel within is a mirror of the cosmic *Shevirah*. The ethical choices we face each day are opportunities to balance the divine energies of Mercy and Judgment. Our relationships are chances to practice *tzimtzum*, the holy act of making space. Our longing for connection is the echo of the *Shekhinah*'s own yearning for union. The work we do in the world, the families we raise, and the communities we build are all potential workshops for the mending of the universe. To live the Lurianic vision is to accept this radical responsibility, to walk through life with the awareness that every action, every thought, every intention matters on a cosmic scale. It is to become a conscious agent of healing in a world waiting to be healed.

And yet, for all its intricate detail—its maps of the five worlds, its genealogy of souls, its catalogue of divine names—the Lurianic system remains, at its heart, a mystery. The blueprint is not the building. The map is not the territory. The Ari's teachings are a finger pointing to the moon of ineffable truth; they are not the moon itself. The purpose of this profound and complex architecture is not to be mastered by the intellect alone, but to awaken the soul to a new way of seeing, a new way of being. It is a ladder, built to help us climb, but we must do the climbing ourselves.

To walk the path of restoration that Isaac Luria laid out is to live with a new set of eyes. It is to see the world not as it appears, but as it truly is: a collection of divine sparks longing for home. It is to see every person, including oneself, as a soul on a sacred mission of repair. It is to live with a profound sense of hope, not because the world is perfect, but because its very imperfection is the source of our holy purpose. The work is vast, and our individual contribution may seem small, but it is the accumulation of countless small acts of light that will, in the end, tip the scales and bring about the final, glorious *tikkun*. The Holy Lion of Safed has given us the blueprint; it is up to us to pick up the tools and begin the sacred work of building. The mystery unfolds not in study, but in the trying.

Glossary of Key Terms

- **Ari:** (Hebrew: אריה, "Lion") The acronym for Rabbi Yitzchak (Isaac) Luria Ashkenazi, from *Elohi Rabbi Yitzchak* ("The Godly Rabbi Isaac"). It is his primary title of reverence.

- **Asiyah:** (Hebrew: עשייה, "Action" or "Making") The lowest of the four primary worlds of creation, the physical realm we inhabit. It is the world where divine light is most concealed and where the work of *tikkun* primarily takes place through physical acts.

- **Atzilut:** (Hebrew: אצילות, "Emanation") The highest of the four primary worlds, the realm of the pure *Sefirot* in perfect unity with the divine. It is the archetypal world to which all repaired sparks return.

- **Beriah:** (Hebrew: בריאה, "Creation") The second of the four worlds, situated below *Atzilut*. It is the world of the divine "throne," the realm of pure intellect and archetypal ideas.

- **Ein Sof:** (Hebrew: אין סוף, "Without End") The Kabbalistic term for the Godhead in its absolute, infinite, and unknowable state, before any self-manifestation or creation.

- **Galut:** (Hebrew: גלות, "Exile") In Lurianic terms, not just a historical condition but the metaphysical state of the entire universe after the *Shevirah*, where sparks are exiled from their source.

- **Gilgul:** (Hebrew: גלגול, "Cycle" or "Transmigration") The doctrine of reincarnation. Souls are reborn into the physical world to complete their specific *tikkun* and rectify past failings. Plural: *gilgulim*.

- **Kavvanah:** (Hebrew: כוונה, "Intention" or "Direction") The focused consciousness and specific mystical intention that gives a ritual or ethical act its power to perform *tikkun*. Plural: *kavvanot*.

- **Kelippot:** (Hebrew: קליפות, "Shells" or "Husks") The shards of the shattered primordial vessels. They represent the forces of darkness, opacity, and concealment in the universe. They entrap the fallen holy sparks. Singular: *kelippah*.

- **Nitzotzot:** (Hebrew: ניצוצות, "Sparks") The holy sparks of divine light that were scattered into the lower worlds after the *Shevirah*. The core mission of humanity is to find and elevate these sparks. Singular: *nitzotz*.

- **Nukva:** (Hebrew: נוקבא, "Female") The feminine *partzuf* (divine persona), associated with the *sefirah* of *Malkhut*. She is the divine recipient, often identified with the *Shekhinah* in exile.

- **Partzufim:** (Hebrew: פרצופים, "Faces" or "Personas") The dynamic, restructured configurations of the *Sefirot* that formed after the *Shevirah*. They function as interacting divine personalities (e.g., Father, Mother, Son, Daughter). Singular: *partzuf*.

- **Sefirot:** (Hebrew: ספירות, "Emanations" or "Countings") The ten fundamental attributes or powers through which *Ein Sof* manifests in the created world. They form the structure of the Tree of Life. Singular: *sefirah*.

- **Shekhinah:** (Hebrew: שכינה, "Dwelling" or "Presence") The immanent, feminine presence of God in the world. In Luria's system, she is in exile along with the scattered sparks and yearns for reunion with her masculine counterpart.

- **Shevirat ha-Kelim:** (Hebrew: שבירת הכלים, "The Shattering of the Vessels") The primordial cosmic catastrophe at the dawn of creation where the vessels containing the divine light broke apart, resulting in the broken and exiled state of our world.

- **Tikkun Olam:** (Hebrew: תיקון עולם, "Repair of the World") The sacred task, assigned primarily to humanity, of gathering the fallen sparks, mending the cosmic rupture, and restoring divine harmony to the universe.

- **Tzimtzum:** (Hebrew: צמצום, "Contraction" or "Withdrawal") The primordial act wherein *Ein Sof* withdrew its infinite light "from itself into itself" to create a conceptual void, allowing a finite world to exist.

- **Yetzirah:** (Hebrew: יצירה, "Formation") The third of the four worlds, situated below *Beriah*. It is the world of emotions and the angelic realms, where the intellectual blueprints from above are given specific form and feeling.

- **Yichud:** (Hebrew: יחוד, "Unification") The sacred union, particularly between the masculine and feminine *partzufim* (*Zeir Anpin* and *Nukva*), which is the ultimate goal of *tikkun*. Also refers to meditative practices designed to unify divine names.

- **Zeir Anpin:** (Hebrew: זעיר אנפין, "Small Face" or "Impatient One") The masculine *partzuf* (divine persona) composed of six *Sefirot*. He represents the divine "Son" or "King" who must be reunited with his bride, the *Nukva*.

- **Zohar:** (Hebrew: זהר, "Splendor" or "Radiance") The foundational text of medieval Kabbalah, written in a cryptic Aramaic. The Zohar was the primary source text for Isaac Luria's mystical meditations and revelations.

Printed in Dunstable, United Kingdom